i

c

o

p

e

For more information, find CCM at:

http://copingmechanisms.net

THE FASSBINDER DIARIES

JAMES PATE

Acknowledgements

I would like to thank *Seven Corners* for publishing the following pieces (some in a highly different earlier versions): "Extraction #1," "The Fassbinder Diaries: Day 27," "The Fassbinder Diaries: Day 733," "Imperial Tangos #1," "Imperial Tangos #2," and Imperial Tangos #3."

I would also like to thank *Action Yes* for publishing an early version of "Exhibit B:" and Everyday Genius for publishing "Pig Beach."

But hate is a passion
and that's near to love anyway.

--- Marine Girls
"Tutti lo sanno"

Part One:

The Ascension Of Veronika Voss

Warm Dark and Dark Cold

The first scenes are silent. The footage is grainy, as if the world being shown has gone through a storm of broken glass shards. As if the air has been delicately mangled. There are figures on the ground, squirming, and it is impossible to tell if they are outside or inside. They could be in an abandoned factory or in a very spacious bedroom or in the middle of a meadow in the middle of the night. We are watching them in the dark. I mean we're in the dark ourselves. Dust floats in the light from the projector. It is a warm dark. Outside, there is a cold dark.

The figures squirm as if they were trying to wrest free from their shadows. There is mud and white streaming rivulets. There is grain in the abandoned spaces and white streaming light dripping from the middles.

The director has arranged the scene on two levels: there are things that blink and things that remain still. The light blinks and the mouths of the figures blink and some of the limbs blink back and forth out of the dark areas of the scene into the lighter areas. But some mouths seem to be crusted over. And all of the eyes are crusted over. Or maybe they

11

aren't crusted over. Maybe the figures never had eyes. Maybe only a few had mouths.

The entire factory or bedroom or meadow dripping light from its lips. Or maybe delicate drops of acid have eaten the scene. There are figures on the ground, silently squirming. But it's impossible to tell if they are silent because they are silent or if they are silent because this is a silent film. We are watching them in the dark. It is a black-and-white dark. Outside, it is a black-and-white dark.

The Ecstasy of Mama Roma

One night Franz and Mieze are watching a black-and-white Pasolini film. It is the movie where the mother is a prostitute and the son is a young criminal who eventually dies in jail in the shape of Christ. Not that he is crucified. But the director has made him look crucified. His arms are out and his face is a slice of bronze reflecting a distant light.

Mieze after the movie says _____, and Franz after the movie replies _____. The curtains are closed. The curtains are the color of blood cells.

And later that night they are in bed, Franz with a beer resting on his stomach, his head on the pillow, his eyes on the ceiling, Mieze on the edge of the bed polishing one of her boots, she is whistling, he is trying to figure out what song it is, it sounds familiar, but he can't, no he can't figure out the tune, and he doesn't ask her. Mieze looks up at Franz and thinks about the last scene of the film, the way the film suddenly goes blank, suddenly goes white, it made her think of that line by Percy Bysshe Shelley, the one about the bright singular white light of eternity, something like that, something along those lines, she can't remember precisely.

13

A window in Berlin. A train in Chicago inching toward at a halt. A thread of black smoke rising in a certain scene in Memphis. Toward numerous night skies.

Return of the Holy Beasts

I was watching the film about the Catholic school, a French film with atrocious subtitles. I was twelve and in the living room of an otherwise empty house.

I was of a certain age. I had recently turned a certain age. There were dripping noises inside one part of my head and red thoughts inside the other. There was salt in my mouth I couldn't spit out. There was sand in my head I couldn't brush away. The curtains were closed. The carpet was pink. The lights were out. The wallpaper was yellow.

In the movie the fierce nun spanks the demure student. Or maybe that's the Japanese movie, the one where the evil old nuns make the pretty young nun take off her blouse. Where the fierce older nuns then tie a crown of thorns around her torso. *The School of the Holy Beasts.* A film I saw in Chicago, in a theater where I had snuck in Vietnamese sandwiches.

I was twelve or twenty-two. In one dark room or a later one. The Japanese nun hiking through the French woods. The French boy jerking-off under a blossoming cherry tree.

15

Having arrived at the age where a fine violet shade lingered in my head. Where I imagined other shades in other heads. Nights heavy as damp sand and nights light as drifting sand. The scene in the French film where the shivering rain-soaked girl finds the Nazi flag in her father's drawer. The taste of pork and cilantro in the silent and serious and ever alert theater.

And the curtains remained closed. And the stand of the lamp remained orange and curved. And the chair containing myself continued to be crimson and heavily stuffed. And the wallpaper even in the dimness consisted of yellow flowers from which countless animals stared.

Retroactive Nights

Could it have ever been resolved retroactively? Not very easily. So we went to Naples. It was fun and tiring and boring and scary and hot and noisy and occasionally windy and perpetually dusty. We temporarily had some money because of X, not much, but enough for two maybe three weeks. When the sun fell it kept falling. When night arrived it kept arriving. That was how things played out there. Or that was my thinking at the time. The men were scraps of wind with red dots inside. The women were noises emitted from a crisp red light. Could it have ever been resolved retroactively? Not very easily. So we grew hot and noisy and our heads turned windy, a breeze hazy with dust. There was a man begging by the train station. He looked like Jesus, had Jesus been fat. Dante stood in the middle of a piazza with trash at his feet and graffiti on the shops around him. We had coffee across the street, under the palm trees. One of us wondered how many people had been killed in Pompeii. None of us knew the answer. It was fun and boring and tiring and scary, like red lights, and then purple lights. Our heads sizzled fatly in the sun. Could it have ever been resolved retroactively? No, not very easily. So I had dreams that turned me inside out, dreams that tended toward red fields, and then purple valleys, toward thighs the color of tongue, dreams that left me gasping for more much as I feared them, dreams inside of red rooms, dreams behind purple curtains. I was a red fish, with a purple spear in my throat. In Naples we played games. We played games with our fingers and our eyes and our knees. We played devil games and coma games and surgical glove games. We played inferno games and trash games and windy games and dusty games. Could it have ever been resolved retroactively? Not so very easily. Our money continued with a commentary of its own. With a politics of its own. This season of rash investments and ashen expenditures. The higher bills we thought of as X and the lower ones as Y. The taste and therefore vomit of money. So we played with the devil's hand. We played with the devil's palm. We shaved the devil's hair. We saw the porn film with seven devils and nine birds on the small TV in our hostel room. We watched the devil's mouth blink. We watched the devil's cock piss. We watched the devil's cunt piss. We watched the devil's thighs quiver. Could it have ever been resolved retroactively? Not easily. Or that was my thinking at the time. The sun continued to fall behind us, leaving our cold fat in the dark. Our investment sizzled into ash. Most of the shadows stood with their doors open, a fine pink dust blowing through.

3:04

Franz said bite me here, and Mieze bit him there, and Mieze said bite me here, and Franz bit her there. The curtains were closed. They were the color of gray snakeskin. Outside, a war developed in Berlin. A gun fired at Dillinger on a movie screen in Chicago. They were someplace else. The seconds were already ahead of them, waiting with their guns pulled. An alley with no escape.

There was a red light flashing. Both in their heads and out, flashing. There was torturous rampaging music, what Mieze called Egregious Sonic Fuck Music. It sounded like iron hissing in a winter lake. It sounded like cold iron against hot iron. It sounded like cold soil thrown on a cold and gaping mouth.

Mieze said suck me here, and Franz sucked her there, and Franz said suck me here, and Mieze sucked him there. On the walls were paintings of aged and vulnerable and meek and sultry cherubs that looked like dirtied candy. Between Franz and Mieze were many angels and demons. Their eyes blinked. Their mouths blinked. The cold and gaping seconds.

An egregious room. An alley room. A Dillinger room.

His hair, she thought, felt like the feathers of a dead bird, the dusty feathers of road-kill. Her hair, he thought, felt like a wig hanging from the crown of a nude tree, a wig with an extinct color and a texture yet to be invented.

After the flashing, the biting, the sucking. After the soil, the cold, the gaping mouth. After the iron, the wig, the candy, and the cherubs. Afterwards Mieze took a sip from the whiskey bottle and peered out the window. The sheets were purple. The scratches and bites on their skin were purple. The purple of dark lipstick. The purple glow thrown from muted televisions playing at 3:04 in the morning. And a car passed by the house. And a car passed by the house. And a car passed by the house. And a car passed by the house.

Q #1:

Where was Fassbinder born?

Q #2:

What was his first homosexual encounter?

Q #3:

What was his first heterosexual encounter?

Q #4:

What was his favorite Jean Genet novel?

Q #5:

What was his favorite line from a Douglas Sirk Film?

Q #6:

How did he die?

Q #7:

What was found on his body at the time of death?

Q #8:

What was found in his body at the time of death?

The Double Life of Mick Jagger

I.

There was this one time at a party in Detroit, this Christmas party. In 2003 or 2004. I was in the bathroom washing my hands and two women walked by outside and one said to the other that the other night she'd had a dream where Mick Jagger was trying to seduce her, except in the dream he was a woman. The other woman outside the door said he was a kind of woman. His mouth, she said, was a kind of vagina. And that exchange made me want to write a poem about that idea. About Mick Jagger's vagina. I tried it the next day. My window overlooked a pawnshop with a shitload of lights flashing in the window. I came up with a poem about a couple, a man and a woman, and they both looked like Mick Jagger, and in a sense they both were Mick Jagger.

II.

In the hotel room in the poem the female Jagger will dress the male Jagger in whore clothes, call him whore names. The male Jagger will think during such episodes of how the meat inside of him could build a massive cathedral should it ever be extracted from his body. That is, if you took the meat and pounded it flat. And used quite a bit of metal wiring. His eyes could be in the center of the cathedral either in the floor and looking up or in the ceiling and staring down. Either way they would never blink. And his teeth. What could they do with his teeth.

III.

You fuck, the female Jagger will say, like a whore. You fuck, the male Jagger will say, like a porn film with the furniture scratched out.

IV.

Yet they do not know they are part of the same person. They do not realize their separate essences will only be reunited upon death.

V.

I was rereading *Helter Skelter* around this time. I was listening to some of the songs from the Manson family around this time, pretty songs sung by young women with childlike and fairylike voices. The two Mick Jaggers would be killed by a hitchhiking serial killer, a thug with a red mohawk. They would die on a bright June morning, in the silence of an Iowa cornfield. Did I hate them, the two Jaggers? I did not hate them. But I liked to think that in some way they hated each other.

VI.

The crows will eat the hearts of the Mick Jaggers. Plastic crows. Lipstick hearts.

A Brief History of the Beatles

Mieze said to me earlier in the week that as a teenager she'd been obsessed with the possibility that Paul really was dead, that the rumor from the 60s had been right after all, that a bland fake Paul had for decades lived under the name and sign of the actual boyish and endearing Paul, and that the most haunting lyrics from any song ever was probably *I Buried Paul* murmured during the end of "Strawberry Fields Forever."

Mieze said to me later in the week that "Helter Skelter" was the song that turned into a crime that turned into a made-for-TV movie.

Revolution Number Nine

Mieze sits on the hotel bed smoking a cigarette.
By her knee is an ashtray and a pair of sunglasses.
She has recently showered.
Her hair is wet and her cheeks are flushed.
She is tired and sunburned and excited and hungry.
Franz is under the covers pretending to be asleep.
Franz listens to himself breathing.
He is tired and sunburned and drifting and hungry.
From the room next door comes music.
It is a low murmur.
Franz can barely hear it.
Mieze can hear it a little better.
She is younger and less sleepy.
The Beatles.
One of the ballads from The White Album.
The television glows.
The screen shows 7,000 figures writhing in the mud.
Or 8,000.
Because the picture is grainy it could be a cartoon.
A cartoon drawn in a crudely realist style.
Or the actors could be electrified mannequins.
And therefore not even alive.
And therefore not even dead.
Many wear black masks and black gloves.
A midnight ball strewn across the mud.
An evening dance left out in the rain.
The ballad ends. "Revolution No. 9" begins.
The curtains are closed.
The curtains are the color of dried rose petals.
The sun is out.

The sun lights the curtains.
Franz thinks it is around four in the afternoon.
Mieze thinks it is around two in the afternoon.

Extraction #1

The man without air used his stomach muscles to center himself in the middle of the field. He used his jaw muscles to extinguish certain ideas he had only come to understand recently. He used his skull muscles to watch films involving parades of pork moving through cities of delicate snow. He used his spine muscles to extract newer and drier shadows from a previously dribbling haze. Behind the purple curtain the 19th century withdrew. Behind the scarlet curtain Marilyn Monroe prepared for the Day of the Dead Mass. Behind the coarse curtain the sea tossed about like houses tumbling from clouds.

The man was dead and had recently been stuffed with salt and black feathers. The part of him that had been dead longest heard voices that whispered from a closet stuffed with white and lemon dresses. The part of him that had been alive furthest waited for the dresses to melt so he could lick their drippings from the floor.

Neither the alive nor dead part had ever waited longer than cloth. Neither the longest nor the furthest had grown past the customary whisperings.

But other sounds continued. The soundtrack dealt with 17 recurrent noises. Other recordings played through the foggier arenas. The wolves made volcano noises. The owls made bone noises. The snakes made June noises. The vultures made scarlet noises. The panthers made soundtrack noises. The bears made lunar noises. The butterflies made gunfire noises.

Demon Flower

But soon afterwards I found myself dating this woman who played in this punk band, this group called Demon Flower. I can't remember when we met but it must've been around Christmas that year because I remember that New Year's Eve we'd been planning on going to this party downtown but ended up screwing the whole night instead and I had had just gotten out of the military and she'd just gotten out of an awful job in some shit town and Dick Clark, he was counting down the final few seconds of that year and she was standing on the bed against the wall and I was kneeling in front of her rubbing my face between her legs, and here I was, just out of the military, just right out of it, and there she was, no longer in a shit job and in a shit town. Then one year ended and one began. One night ended and another began. And millions of years had already ended and millions more were waiting. Each like an unmade bed. Each like a night in a shit town you never heard of. Each like a cot with a thin clean blanket. She stood there, her back against the wall, and I knelt there rubbing my face between her legs and licking and feeling, I don't know why, but feeling like a cat. There was no new year and no old year. But there were some years and then other years. And the military. And the other militaries. And the shit jobs, and shit towns.

U-Bahn

I'm on the train under Berlin. I'm on the speckled train. The strangers look like gardens full of glass shards. They look like graffiti from a fading silent film. I'd had this dream before. The first part was a wall. The second involved a door that stared out into a cluster of blood clots.

I was on the train, waiting. There were other parts of the dream waiting too. The strangers calculated one ride for every cloud in purgatory, one feather from every rubble, one sea for every beach. The strangers examined their hair and their hair and their mouths and their mouths. Under the lights they were naked the way rust is naked. They made sounds like cities passing over into sleep. Like subways with the brakes missing. They'd dreamt about their mouths for centuries. They swallowed over and over, to prove they had tongues. They blinked to prove they had skulls. They bit one hand among the many.

Visibility in the Catatonic Room.

We watched others play ourselves on the television. They were zombies with glue for faces or figures of glue with flat eyes. They waited for a cloud to trust in the vast blue noise. They disrobed except for their watches. When they were done with each other they drank wine and devoured cold chicken legs in the tangled and ghostly and champagne-colored sheets. I hear, among other things, your fingers with their crowns of blood. Among other things, a crown of dried air, another impulse toward frescos of shit.

The Fassbinder Diaries: Day 1

The film critic returned to his apartment and checked his email and finished the last piece of chocolate mousse cake in the refrigerator and took a bath during which he listened to the couple argue next door. The film critic squeezed lemon over a salad that included spinach, tuna, and red onion. The film critic returned to the lobby of the hotel just as night was falling. The film critic brushed her teeth while standing in the den watching a scene from *2001: A Space Odyssey*. The film critic told the woman he'd met at the bar that his uncle had been close to John Ford and even though it was not true it was quite a relief to say it. The film critic walked down a hallway that seemed to go on for more than a year. The film critic took his cellphone from his jacket with his heart beating wildly, his hands trembling. The film critic walked around St. Louis with a gun in her jacket as if expecting an event of possibly tragic proportions. The film critic slept. The film critic turned his face to the wall. The film critic poured another shot of bourbon and lowered herself into the bathtub, into the sudsy water. The film critic watched *2001: A Space Odyssey* every Christmas Eve and had been doing so since he was twenty-three.

The Fassbinder Diaries: Day 27

The film critic tosses a slice of tuna to his orange and slender and expectant cat. The film critic argues with her mother while watching Klaus Kinski stride about in the rain, violet flashes of lightning in the mountains behind him. The film critic walks through one hallway after another, hearing a cellphone ring behind a distant door. The film critic dresses up as a dead Marilyn Monroe for Halloween. The film critic pours a bottle of wine over her bed while arguing with her husband over the phone, it saturates the sheets, it dribbles on the wood floor. The film critic plays a Johnny Cash CD during intercourse with the woman he met at a midnight showing of *Liquid Sky*. Behind them is a table with four empty cans of beer and a deck of old Soviet playing cards. The film critic cuts her hair in the mirror. She cuts it short. Then shorter. From an apartment across the alley comes the sound of salsa music playing. It is 3:12 in the morning.

Part Two:

Fassbinder's first theatrical production at a farm in southern Germany

Pig knot

Records spin. Flabby skin. Pigs feed. Full of greed.
--- Bush Tetras
"Snakes Crawl"

The pig is born as a bleat.
The pig is a knot of bleating sound.
The pig is the knot in the dark.
The pig is shivering in the dark.
The pig is smart.
The pig has a human wail and the pig has a human tongue.
The pig is the first noise.
The pig will be the last noise.
I am fond of pig parties.
I have been to many pig parties.
I have stood in the corner of pig parties, drinking tequila.
I have heard what they say about the flesh at pig parties.
I have heard what they say about the meat inside the skull.
The pig is said to resemble a thick kiss or a red kiss.
Or a yellow kiss.

Or a rose kiss.
I've been to pig parties where the walls have been the loveliest
pink.
I have worn the masks and I've listened to the whispers.
And I've heard the stories of war spew at pig parties.
I've felt the dampness inside those parties.
I've smelled the ash that remains from those parties.
I've heard of the smoke that appears from no apparent fire.

Pig Radio

There was always Pig Radio.
You can hear it later in the night.
When I listen I think of angels in pink surgical gowns.
I think of shaved cats that look like small pigs.
I think of shaved human heads that look like starved pigs.
I think of thin kisses followed by thick kisses.
I think of the parts of us that spew.
There are so many parts of us capable of spewing.
Maybe there will be more parts soon.
Parts capable of spewing further and further.
At some point we could spew and spew.

I want to leave the thickest of pink stains behind.

Pig Spew

The pig is the cause of war spew.
Or rather, the pig is the dream that ends in war spew.
I'm neither here nor there.
I've been at parties, thinking of something else entirely.
There were countless noises coming from Pig Radio.
Some of those noises are human.
Some are thought to have once been human.
But they could have been human long ago.
Pig Radio itself reveals nothing.
Pig Radio thinks of something else entirely.
The paradox of war is both here and there.
Or rather, the noises are Pig Radio entirely.

Pig Pink

If only the singular pig could once regard the plural.
If only a plurality of pigs would withstand.
I've been to pig parties as silent as redder hours.
I've seen the pink masks and the thick masks.
I've touched the eyeholes and the mouthholes.
I've been to pig parties with their spew of hours.
The taste of the pig is counter to the spew of pig.
And the night of pig chews the day of the pig.
And the day of pig chews the night of the pig.
Pig Radio with its singular regard for the thicker kisses.
Pig Night with its infinite regard for the hours.

Pig Wings

A pig can vibrate upon birth.
A pig can thicken upon birth.
A pig can gnaw through upon birth.
A pig can drain exclusively upon birth.
A pig can attend the pig party.
But not all parties involve the pig.
When I listen to pigs I think of pig angels.
Angels with pink meaty wings.

Wings and the most translucent of bones.

Pig Brink

The night of the pig is there from the first day.
The day of the pig is there from the first day.
But Pig Radio is there before the first day.
Pig Radio is there after the last day.
Pig Radio, with its subtle noises.

Pig Radio, with its non-subtle noise.

Pig Beach

The noise in the pig. The pig in the noise.
The time for pig time.
The end of the start of pig time.
The time of the pig thorn.
The mouth drooling in the heart of the pig thorns.
The heart drooling in the shape of the pig.
The hour of the pig light. The arson in the pig dark.
The noise of the pig in the human head.
The noise of the human in the pig head.
The pig fever in the human brain.
The pig light in the human eye.
The pig eye in the dark staring.
The lemon of the pig. The glory and run-off of the pig.
The pig wall alone on the human beach.
The human sand pink and the pig wall burnt.
The human hand scurrying in the pig night.
The mouth drooling in a human night.
The hour of the pig hour.
The hour of the blood drool.
The hour of the pig drool slipping from the light into the
dark.
The human spew in the pig head.
The human dark in the pig light.
The peeled lemon of the pig. The hour of the pig lemon.
The crown of pig thorns on the pink sand.
The beach light bright in the pig eye.

45

Part three:

mother kusters
Pirouetting
in the Filmlight

One Summer Continuous Hot and Claring #1

I.

But the problem was something else entirely. So everyone suggested. I was broke and took the café job. The place had been called ___ for many years but it had been bought by two elderly and craven and sunburned hippies and turned into ___. Its walls were blue. Its two sofas were crimson. Its noise registered as a ceaseless hum. Its windows bright even on rainy days. I hated and actually kind of despised the entire customer service aspect of the job, the taking of orders and the making of coffee, even though I love coffee, even though I continue to love coffee despite my eventual aversion to it that balmy and rainy summer, both the taste and the smell, the taste and smell of coffee, and even the grounds, the black dense coffee grounds, their look of black dense earth, denser and blacker than the blackest and densest of earth. And the rain that summer wandered in and wandered in. The rain smell. The rain hum. The blue and ever dense hum of summer rain. The clattering across the roof and the clattering across the windows. A noise heard from both ends of a film, the beginning as well as the end, two anonymous sounds shifting imperceptibly toward one another.

II.

But the problem was something else entirely. So everyone suggested at the time. The café had white chairs and these white ceiling fans and some days I'd come in stoned and stare at those fans and it was like they were hypnotizing me, stretching the afternoons out until you could almost hear them snap. Ever so gently and gingerly snap. Most days weren't so bad. Most days weren't what I would call awful. Most days I drank more and more espresso and returned to my apartment so wired the blood in my head was sizzling. Crackling. A crackling that reminded me of radio static, a static through which I might hear a stranger's voice, a static through which I might see a red light flashing in the sonic distance.

III.

But the problem was something else entirely. So everyone at the time suggested. The whole world rotting and the President stupid and wars and wars and that summer hot and glaring. Anger followed by wistfulness followed by erotic expectations followed by a chilly June haze followed by a Monday of alternating storm-light. I ever so gingerly and I ever so gently. My life a film nobody including myself wanted to cast. Most days stretched and sizzled. A café with blue walls in which rain was falling. The weather ever more clattering and dense.

One Summer Continuous Hot and Claring #2

I'd talk to my friend Maria. I'd talk on the phone to my friend Maria. I'd ask my friend Maria about the Thai or Iranian or Russian films she'd seen the night before. I'd ask my friend Maria about lifeless bars she'd gone to recently or the relentless songs she'd heard. My friend Maria was my best friend that very lengthy and balmy and rainy and unexpected and unnerving and hirsute summer. My friend Maria was like an eclipse. My friend Maria could have been said to be at least one eclipse. My friend Maria as that moment in a film where the soundtrack includes nothing but hedges blowing and distant traffic. My friend Maria as the furthest echo. My friend Maria wore blue summer dresses and white summer dresses and orange summer dresses and black summer dresses and a black summer dress with a few pink ribbons and an orange summer dress with a creamy lacy collar. My friend Maria wore black boots and red sneakers and white sneakers but never sandals not even on the hottest and longest and most unnerving of days. My friend Maria had orange summer dresses and a way of holding a cigarette that continued to. My friend

Maria telling me that in the convergence of the life-less and relentless many passions would. My friend Maria participated in at least one of the summer eclipses. The tongue dreams my friend Maria alluded to. The song my friend Maria ended up writing near the closing credits. My friend Maria said no not right now maybe in the fall because of. My friend Maria said head games come in all sorts of, all kinds of. My friend Maria in the black spot of an eclipse. In the blank second of an opposing hour. In the invisible corner of an otherwise rain. The hirsute and unnerving summer my friend Maria had heard rumors of. The summer rain in which my friend Maria will have left her softer sneakers.

One Summer Continuous Hot and Claring #3

We would drink and argue and smoke up and argue and argue and smoke up and orange thoughts with lemon smears would occur concurrently and crimson weather with feathered edges and the redder angels without noise and once she made pork chops in a gigantic heavy and weathered pan and once around 3:43 am and once I heard You aren't even in the running said possibly outside the window possibly on TV and once made a stir-fry and drank icy mint juleps and we would smoke up and argue but we didn't employ overly personal or demeaning or stereotypical or cheaply advantageous insults and the redder angels without their conventional fur and the redder weather without noise and drink and smoke up and watch feverish television roiling with its fevered noise and a few wonderful and feverish films and while pork chops browned and while chicken sizzled and while drinks were poured and while ice melted and dripped down our legs and concurrently the orange and redder thoughts and argue and argue and the terrible hours and the fevered hours and the reddest expanse of the noisy angels during the more lemony hours and the chicken on the chopping board and several pieces and the ground meat she sizzled in the gigantic heavy pan and pink to gray and gray to brown and around 3:43 am and argue and argue and naked and overly personal.

One Summer Continuous Hot and Claring #4

There were these nights that summer. Then further nights. And the forgotten nights. A few miles outside Memphis. The nights I've attempted to forget. The nights that felt as if they'd already forgotten me even as I walked through them. The humid stark nights and the nights that emptied out into larger and more terrifying nights like thoughts flowing toward later and more terrifying thoughts. And something else entirely, always something else. I crashed at her place more then a few times and her at mine too. A few minutes outside the city. Our longest talks on those nights with us in bed and the ceiling. Our most private moments with us in the kitchen and the windows. Our most careful moments with us swimming and the radio. She taking a course on ancient China that summer, and me asking about their empires, where they went to or what remained of them in the books she read, the tests she took.

One Summer Continuous Hot and Claring #5

But was any finalizing outcome forthcoming? One morning in August we went to this neighbor's pool and they were in some European town or another and took off everything but our underwear and listened to their radio and made mojitos from their supplies. But was any finalizing outcome forthcoming? I listened mostly to old music, Ray Charles, some of Dylan's super early shit, a few scratchy blues records, the singers' voices like water dripping from leaves after the rain has already passed, and also scary Russian music, glacial Russian music, the harsher more radiant side of Shostakovich, eerie Russian symphonies like angelic flickers in the dark summer sky. But was any finalizing outcome forthcoming? There was an old man at the café, a homeless man, his shirt and hair were filthy, he used to come in once a week, and I'd see him open little plastic packets of ketchup he'd gotten from some McDonald's or Burger King, and he'd eat the ketchup on the café patio, his hands trembling, his beard stained red. But was any finalizing outcome forthcoming? That summer, I got a tattoo. I took a road trip to New Orleans and got this

Asian dragon tattoo. That summer, I watched a film about a night that never ended and I read about a book about a sun that never set, but only hovered near the edge of the horizon at midnight, waiting to return. But was any finalizing outcome forthcoming? The gloves with gnawed fingers on the café table, an early Bob Dylan song playing in the back, possibly the kitchen. But was any finalizing outcome forthcoming? The midnight sun at the edge. The man with shaking hands opening small red packets. The hands raising each packet to his lips. The moon never setting. The café never closing.

One Summer Continuous Hot and Claring #6

I asked her what did she like better, Confucian thought or Taoist thought. I asked her when did they start to build the Great Wall of China. I asked her when did they complete the Great Wall of China. I asked her what would a Chinese farm have looked like a thousand years ago. I asked her what would a Chinese palace have looked like two thousand years ago. And sometimes she was on the phone with me. And sometimes she was in the room next to the one I sat in, dyeing her hair. And mostly it was Taoist thought, though once or twice it was Confucian.

Q #1:

Where was Petra von Kant born?

Q #2:

What was her first homosexual encounter?

Q #3:

What was her first heterosexual encounter?

Q #4:

What was her favorite Jean Genet novel?

Q #5:

What was her favorite line from a Douglas Sirk Film?

Q #6:

How did she die?

Q #7:

What was found on her body at the time of death?

Q #8:

What was found in her body at the time of death?

Certain Intermittent Effects

She started writing one day and she started writing one hour and she started writing one night. Her hand in an empty house. Or rather a house empty except for carpets and furniture and a few stray dishes. This was the fourth day of June, 2002. What is writing? It might be a red thought followed by a series of intermittent violet effects. Or a lemon smear in a circle of quivering red sensations. Or an isle of desire in a turbulent lake of nausea. She began writing her dreams, especially the ones with gaunt cheeks and extravagant hair. She started writing down her dimmer memories, especially those that took place in hotels with dirty carpets that lingered too long by the highway. The fall she spent in Baltimore, the night she lost her shoes in Tucson. She could ask her boyfriend about his first sexual experiences and when he was at work she could write those experiences down in great detail. She could write down her own first sexual experiences. She could write down what she wished her first sexual experiences had actually been instead of what they actually were. This was the seventh day of May, 2008. What is writing? A soft noise followed by a softer noise. A red light intrigued by a redder light. She could write the same word over and over again, a random word picked from the dictionary. She could copy scenes from famous novels but add her own name for certain words, such as "rain" or "thunderous." She could find her copy of the *Epic of Gilgamesh* and write out the dream dreamt by Gilgamesh's spiritual brother Enkidu, the one involving the dark house of death where the dwellers eat clay, and she could extend the scene, making the house larger and larger until it took in entire nations, entire empires. What is writing? A red smear in an empty house, an isle covered with bird shit.

Chekhov's Firearm

The woman who played my torso and the man who played my tongue and the flayed rabbit that played my heart and the flayed rabbit that played my brain and the wall with flecks of shit on it that played my chest and the million tongues of grass licking at nothing that played my hair and the scorched dollhouse that played my genitalia and the suicidal movie star that played my lungs and the electrical outlet that played my mouth waited in the field for me to fire my gun.

The Fassbinder Diaries: Day 364

The film critic searches in the dewy weeds for her glasses. The sky above her spotted by pink and purple clouds. The film critic in silk pajamas tapes a postcard of a Neapolitan skull over his stricken and comatose desk. Outside it is snowing, great gusts of it swirling against the black mirror of the window. The film critic stands in a patch of tiger lilies looking for the switchblade a boyfriend had given her on her sixteenth birthday. The film critic feels the hair on his legs twitch in the dark. She wears a red raincoat and is thinking about the canvases Edward G. Robinson paints in *Scarlet Street*, works with jagged shadows and smashed daylight, his heart a charred wad of leftover beef. The film critic watches a short film in a cold movie theater, his eyes lit like city streetlamps. His memory occasionally feels like a series of white walls on a beach, their bottom halves puckered by gunfire and their upper halves faded by continual daylight. The film critic wears an emerald robe with a dragon on its back as she searches in the grass for the slender gin-flavored cigar she has dropped. She is twenty-three and thirty-six and forty-one and her most recent nightmares flash with a glacial light.

The Fassbinder Diaries: Day 733

The film critic passed by in the back seat of a blue Pontiac at the age of six, the radio playing, with the desert all around her. She counted cacti shadows until she fell asleep. Her forehead was warm, the window cold. The film critic drank Jim Beam as he rode quickly around on his bike, searching for the right address, or a part of the town that looked familiar. A bird chirped in a film set centuries ago, along the leafy outer boroughs of an empire. In the film critic's most recent dream she made love to a high school boyfriend on a bed that was really the desert, a pink desert consisting of salt instead of sand. It burned their eyes and mouths and scraped away at their bare skin. Under their skin was a landscape of irregular beauty, like layers of stained marble. The film critic bought another postcard from the only café that remained opened in the town. A faded postcard and an empty café. In the backseat of a blue Pontiac, the radio going, shadows to the left and wind coming from the right. The angular paintings by Edward G. Robinson in *Scarlet Street*, the naked girl forced to eat shit with a fancy spoon in *Salò*. The first scenes in the film unfolding during a never changing dusk. The film critic talked to her mirror, the film critic spoke with his cat.

Footage

The film critic touched the blank spot where her thoughts continued to appear: the itchy thoughts and the ugly thoughts and the thoughts with pierced and stricken faces.

Part Four:

The Crucifixion Of Maria Braun

Winter Dance

Mieze is in a white summer dress and battered parka, she wears a red wig, a wig with curls at the shoulder, she hasn't worn a wig in years and she is not sure why she is wearing one tonight, she is beside the jukebox dancing to Ray Charles. There is an icy winter light in her thoughts and a breezy winter night outside and a paper moon in the sky and an endless shadowy road extending through her mind. There is a voice singing in the middle of the hour. The voice of Ray Charles or someone who used to be called Ray Charles.

Franz is sitting in a chair, he is in jeans and a Nina Hagen T-shirt, and in his right pocket is a pack of gum, and in his left are his keys and a lighter and one joint and a notebook that includes the directions to a party they might or might not go to later in the evening. His hands have thought of other types of rooms. His left knee is scarred from a bike accident that occurred at the age of seventeen and his other knee is already in another town with other rooms, dreaming among other and warmer knees.

The bar window shining in the middle of the voice. Ray Charles singing from another millennium. The winter dance. The parka and wig and white summer dress dance. The ghost party dance. Mieze with two drunken arms raised and tongue tingling. Franz at the party he will never go to nor hear stories of nor forget about. The jukebox surrounded by winter air.

midnight movies

The mouth will swallow the finger. Then the next finger. Then the rest of the hand. The air will blow through the window and the sleeves. The siren sound will move through the wind and branches and the thoughts near the edge of town. The grass will grow through the fingers and out of the mouth. The film will play. The film has already played. Trees in the foreground and wind through the branches and wind against the theater walls. The mouth in the movie being red and anonymous and stricken. The mouth being old and homeless and chapped. The mouth surrounded by beard and wet melting snow. The thoughts blowing from the edges of the movie, torches lit, the villagers gathering.

Fat

In the garden small pockets of fat appeared under the trees. They quivered in the light and vibrated in the film. Then the pockets turned into fatty mouths. They salivated. They were fleshy and wormy and slick. None of us knew why or what they wanted or what thoughts they'd had or what memories they'd pursued in order to arrive here.

My girlfriend spent her most private hours whispering prayers in Pig Latin. Her gods were named after extinct flowers. There were televisions in our house tuned to the Red channel. It glowed with its red light. She lingered by the window and watched the garden grow extended tangles of hair. She ate fat and digested fat. I ate fat and digested fat. But other fats returned. Other hair and their memories. Pockets with saliva in the corners.

Another man loved her but we knew he was dead and often missing. His face quivered in the light of the airier gods. He said her shoulder was a gristle party. He said her hair had been longer than centuries. He said in Baltimore the last of spring. In New York the remainder of the fall. Our house digesting both fat and the memory of fat and gods growing hair in our corners.

She broke a mirror with her heel and left marks of blood for us to follow. The games consisted of screw-drivers and falsified Indian folklore and stories of slaves making slasher films in the forest, their shirts like clouds in a greased sky. We wondered how long we could sleep in a sleepless house and how much fat we could digest before the memory of fat faded.

The man who loved my girlfriend claimed to be a dying fish gasping in the middle of the floor and an untold chronicle of Christ and the meatiest part of Plato's afterbirth. He warned us Plato's sperm glowed in his mouth, the money shot of wisdom. And the fat thickening in the Baltimore sun and the fat glistening in the New York sun.

Garden of Whores and Jackals

The slow accumulation of capital continued unabated. There was nothing any of us could do about it. But I suspected things were bad. Bad and getting worse. My wife gave me a car antenna for Christmas. And a gutted radio for the new year. And broken earphones for my birthday. And a dull record needle for Easter. But that's how things played out that year. That's how things were, when I think back on it. She'd lock herself up in our bedroom and yell at me, calling me a whore and a jackal. The slow accumulation of wealth continued unabated. There was nothing any of us could do about it. Did we continue to have sexual intercourse? Yes, but as if some god or demon possessed our bodies during the act, our bodies and part of our minds. A red demon or a yellow and icy god. We had a new car, at least it was new to us, this blue Cadillac. We'd drive through the night sometimes, or at least until one or two in the morning. We'd drive all through the city. Good neighborhoods. Not-so-good neighborhoods. Some of the houses looked like there were whole families lying dead inside, shot up. The slow accumulation of capital continued unabated. There was nothing any of us could do about it. And then if you're like me you start to think what if it was true, what if there really is a family in that house all shot up. And what if one of them is a little bit alive, a grandmother whose small finger, the one on her left hand, is ever so slightly twitching. The slow accumulation of capital continued unabated. There was nothing any of us could do about it. There were hot nights and breezy nights and nights so still it was like you could hear a twig break and cooler nights and nights that felt like they'd happened a hundred years ago and nights that felt like they were being dreamt up by someone lying in bed, someone you didn't even know, someone you did not ever want to know, and nights where the sky completely opened up, and nights that smelled like earth, that had that muddy smell, and nights that came from nowhere and nights that would go nowhere, and hot nights and breezy nights and nights so still it was like you could hear a twig break and cooler nights and nights that felt like they'd happened a hundred years ago and nights that felt like they were being dreamt up by someone lying in bed, someone you didn't even know, someone you did not ever want to know, and nights where the sky completely opened up, and nights that smelled like earth, that had that muddy smell, and nights that came from nowhere and nights that would go nowhere, and hot nights and breezy nights and nights so still it was like you could hear a twig break.

Exhibit A:

The film critic is driving through white nights and black days, through red cities with nothing but empty sidewalks and windows. She reaches an appropriate place to stop. It looks like a prison that had once been a ballroom. It seems to be a school with its brains knocked out.

She walks through an infinite white corridor, until she reaches the funeral. The casket is full of the blackest coffee. The service includes chairs and three doors that lock from the inside.

She is the only one present so far. Though there are a few figures of clay in some of the chairs. And figures of moist velvet on other chairs. Some of the figures are shaped like heads, though most are torsos, and there are a few legs shivering. All of the figures look like they have only recently been brought inside from sitting out in a rain of ash.

The film critic wears a red scarf. Her husband tells her it looks like her throat has been slashed. She wears a blue scarf and her sister says her head appears to levitate in air.

The sound of the film continues in the next room. There's always a film in the next room, the film critic thinks. The voices could be rain that falls without hitting either foreground or background. The voices are not talking to her but through her and she is trying to listen but not hear them.

Exhibit x:

The figure without arms licks the figure without a tongue and the figure with hands but no fingers caresses the back of the figure with no head. The lemon air around them is haunted by crimson voices. The breeze around them has poured through a century of painterly silence.
The figure with no head is only good for breathing. So the director had decided.

The figure without hair probes part of its thinner shoots into the soft patches of the figure without brains and the figure with only a few branches of meat curls around the figure that consists of pink mist.

There will be crimson voices to reconsider. There might have been at least one century without tongues or hair or brain. The lemon figure might be called water and the crimson figure could well be sand.

They are on a beach. The breezier figures pour through the upper branches of air. It is a dark night, a silent night, a contracting night, a weathered night, an airy night, a night haunted by the general figure of night. So the director had decided. So will the figures lick and be licked. So will the silence pour. So will the meat crimson.

Exhibit B:

The lovers among us sleep like thighs.
The comatose eat sleep like cloud.
And the ghosts that searched our collars and straps.
Their cold feet in the naked closet.
Their roads in the storm closet.
Their grins in the salt closet.
Their tongues in the thorn closet.
Their throats in the iron closet.
Their shoulders in the arson closet.
Their windows in the burnt closet.

Their choirs in the velvet closet.

Exhibit C:

No one brought the mouth among the flowers. No one dragged the torsos nearer. No one could count the number of teeth that had bitten through.

We had been planning a film based on the bonier gods, with their skeleton grins and winter gazes. Withered flowers in different aspects of hair.

Heavens tinted. A multitude of years absent from the scene.

A shaking quaking started behind the emerald door. The more frantic shadows thought of themselves as afterimages from nights bright as milk.

Their Stroking Glove remained inert on the plate, though some of its fingers had been chewed. Their Examination Glove smelled like the newer types of saliva.

The gods with sinew among the flowers. The gods with their torsos exhaling.

The White Hotel

after D.M. Thomas

The biting and sucking near the outermost shrub lasted seven centuries and thirteen seconds. The coughing spell wandered from cave to cave growing colder and more robust. The shadows slept from their skin down. They smelled between their legs. They smelled between repercussions. They smelled excrement in the grass. They smelled shit along the walls that led inside. They smelled fire where their brains used to rest. They smelled hair in distant places. They smelled hot blood and then cooler blood. They smelled burning fat. They smelled mud in the war zone. They had bewildered holidays. They were tremors in the listening gowns. They held wolves open. They slept like mist in the night. They fastened. They fastened tighter. They made the Face of the Melancholy Dog. They maintained an Egyptian doubt. They thought about the dark messages. They thought about the light messages.

Sinners and Saints

I.

The trees are blue and the air red and a terrible beard of thorns grows from your softest lung.

II.

The only thing moving within seventy acres of desert is a forked tongue.

III.

The tree breathes like lungs. The thorns in this film are painted red. The weather will continue to be tinted blue.

IV.

The later parts of the film dealt with the life story of Mick Jagger's tongue.

V.

The crucifixion of Mick Jagger's tongue in Alejandro Jodorowsky's 1980s version of *Our Lady of the Flowers*.

The First House on the Right

The season kept its hands scurrying behind the sad house, the unkempt house, the ninth and eleventh house, the gaunt house, the gutted house, the mangled house, the house with no roof or wall or obligatory history, the house with little else, the house with a single color, the house with a single shadow inside, the house with a single strip of light glowing under its door, the house on the white beach that will never recover, that will never remember, that will never return, the fish flopping on the sand, the swimmers in wet gowns barking at the wind.

Part Five:

The Stiletto Museum
Of Petra von Kant

Imperial Tangos #1

If you look at something long enough, I've discovered, the meaning goes away.

- Andy Warhol

They have arranged it so that the scene takes place in a ballroom. There are countless chandeliers, though only a few are on. There are countless mirrors along the wall, though most are hidden in shadow. And the ones not in shadow are freckled with bird shit.

The dancing couples shift their leaden figures to the leaden orchestration. The purpose is to dance until someone not themselves is either born or laid to rest. The ballroom is lit by a grainy light. The theme of the dance is Extraction. The thinking by the dancers in the ballroom tends toward sockets of grainy light. Others stand near the edge of the scene waiting for the light to flicker out.

One dancer who had once been laid to rest or possibly born is writing in the hotel bed this ugly ugly, this red red, this leaden leaden, this mirror mirror. Her dress wilts in the hot uneven room. Her idea is starting to ache. Yet the ache is not unpleasant. It makes her skin feel like streams of warm milk: milk that drips from the bed and through the floorboards into the room below, where it continues to drip through the floorboards, and so on, until it reaches the sewers.

They have arranged it so that the heads of many of the couples have been hallowed out by extractions. The have arranged it so that the heads of many of the couples have grainy and countless notions pouring from their faces.

Imperial Tangos #2

The endless boulevards extend among endless extractions.

Imperial Tangos #3

The dance is based on the Fassbinder film that has long been laid to rest, its head stuffed with roses. They have found a pink hotel by the cellophane lake, with many pink sugary swans in the distance. They have arranged it so that the dancing takes place from the knees down.

One of the ballroom dancers reads his diary while his lover fucks another dancer in the hotel elevator. They are like a pair of hips almost but not quite born.

The diary consists of scenes in which figures covered with bird shit and gold glitter and clothed by tattered silk stand like statues in a meadow that is really a stage in an abandoned factory. But they soon arrange it so that night falls on the meadow. They dim the factory lights one by one. The lovers in the elevator dry. The clothes in the elevator remain like sunlight.

Another film could have taken place. And maybe it will. Or maybe the film that could have taken place will only consist of a few scenes, and the rest will remain written in diaries and on the backs of napkins and one or two postcards.

The hips approach the mirror and draw back and approach and draw back.

Imperial Tangos #4

One dancer realized she could only have been born. Her idea making the dance ugly ugly.

The others waiting in the corner for the lights to flicker out begin vomiting an almond light of their own. They had arranged it so that the scene is truly and utterly fucked.

The dancing itself is partially asleep as if the orchestration surrounding it had forgotten to misplace its ugly ugly.

The elevator remains on the beach, its mouth ajar and releasing pink mist. The sand on the beach heavy as clay. The sand around the elevator is pink, but it is unclear if it is pink because of the sunset, or because of the pink film lights, or because the sand is really a hillside of pink sugar. The ballroom is empty except for the last extraction.

Imperial Tangos #5

The black wall and a white wall and a carpet of sand between them, a film being made without actors or trees or guns or eyes or headlines, I wanted to be the gravedigger with the blackened smile, you wanted to be a window staring out on to prison yard, a window splattered with cheap cosmetics, we had some things going for us, a mouth twisted by a red thumbprint, part of the snarl flattened, a bared chest covered with goose bumps, a single pale nipple white in the light, a dab of paint with its snout sniffing, shifting. The director an assembly of snouts twitching.

The black wall and the beach and the pad of flesh scratching at the air.

Imperial Tangos #6

So many arms alone in the air. So many thighs blinking in the light. So many hands drying in the weeds. So many necks waiting in the heat. So much hair alone in the basement. So many eyes staring at the wall. The ugly ugly thoughts strewn along the beach. The parade of extractions with their roots dripping. The sunlight piercing through the pink mist like useless noise. The elevator door with its jaw broken and askew. The road of sand leading from the door and through the door and away and toward.

Gods of the Plague #1

And Mieze says yes, she remembers that scene from the Fassbinder film, the one with the gangster with the fatalistic 70s mustache, and his long black leather coat, and his head of prison light, and his thoughts in black-and-white film colors, and the woman who will one day claim to be Maria Braun beautiful in the mirror in the room behind the stage, and the two of them flipping through a porn magazine given to her by the woman from the east who sells secrets.

And Mieze picks up the cold turkey leg while wearing black gloves. The meat is cold and greasy and the room around the meat is clean and cold.

And later that night Mieze says yes, that's right, she had said previously the woman from the east was her favorite character, though she by the end is another victim, and the shock of it is that it's hard to imagine a beautiful woman selling so many secrets could ever be gotten rid of by such a simple fact as a bullet.

And Mieze closes one curtain after another and dresses for work, her night shift at the hospital, or was it the nursing home, and the meat on the table with her teeth marks, and the glass on the table with her lip marks.

Gods of the Plague #2

And Mieze says she was on this hike with a friend of hers, this guy named Tommy, who was really into German film, and who was always making these elaborate and contradictory and paradoxical arguments about why Herzog was better than Fassbinder, except for early Fassbinder, who, he claimed, no one could touch, no one could outdo, like the scene from *Gods of the Plague* where the male criminal is killed in a botched holdup and the female characters stand around his grave like Furies that have been momentarily appeased. And Mieze says she would remind Tommy about how the last thing you remember from the film is the woman who will one day become Maria Braun standing in the cemetery in her beautiful slightly sleazy coat looking into the distance as if looking into the future characters she will one day play. And Mieze says one day while talking about these things, among others, they were hiking through the woods in northwestern Tennessee, and it started to rain, so they ran under a rock near a creek, and as they were sitting there watching the lightning and listening to the thunder they started kissing each other though they had never kissed in the past, it was like they had wandered into another film, had moved from being in a lightweight teenage drama into a soft porn film with multiple scenes in the woods, and soon he was inside of her and her legs were wrapped around his hips, he did not wear a condom and she had not asked him to wear one, though looking back, Mieze says, she doesn't know why, and can only attribute his not wearing a condom and her not asking him to wear one to a stupid youthful belief in spontaneity, though he did pull out when he came, Mieze says, and afterwards they held each other and listened to the rain pour through the tree branches above them, and then they slowly and gingerly, Mieze says, pulled their underwear and jeans back up and without a word about what had happened started to discuss the prequel to Fassbinder's *Gods of the Plague*, a film Mieze thought was entitled *Love is Colder than Death*, though she might have been wrong, and maybe the title was different, maybe love was colder than something else entirely, and Mieze and Tommy both admitted it was a film neither of them had seen, though they intended to in the near or distant future.

Dream of the varying
Pork Cloud

She wept over the dream that sounded like cars crashing in
the sky.
He felt troubled by the dream where faces melted towards
mouths that never closed.

She wore black in the salt dream.
He wore pink to the pork dream.

She walked through the dream located on a beach with ex-
tinct sand.
He screamed in a dream that ended without him.
She called her dreams obscene names.
He could tell his dreams apart from the way they breathed in
his hands.

Mice were a problem of the spirit, rats a problem of the mind.
Tigers presented their meat foliage and panthers their shadow
foliage.

Secrets of the Hollywood Hills
#1

I met Franz in Memphis in late December at a café. It had white tables and white ceiling fans. It had blue walls. It had bright windows. It had a crimson sofa. It had another crimson sofa.

I met Franz in late December. He on the crimson sofa. Myself on a white chair. And a nearby blue wall. A bright window nearby. He had just gotten in from Los Angeles. Sometimes in Los Angeles he had no place of his own and slept on other people's couches. Sometimes, especially after working on a film, he had quite a bit of money. But he made a point of spending it before he could save it.

The crimson sofa with overstuffed and threadbare armrests and with feet carved to look like talons holding balls. The blue walls bare. The ceiling fans spinning. A warm December day.

He told me he was helping out on this low-budget film in Tucson back around Halloween, he told me it was a great city but they were filming in this cramped little apartment in a bad neighborhood, meth dealers were always on the corner trying to look like they were just hanging out, sometimes helicopters circled at night, when you came in from a party say around two or so you prayed you wouldn't get shot or held up, but the desert he said, the desert.

Secrets of the Hollywood Hills #2

Franz told me that afternoon at the cafe that he would talk to Mieze on his cell phone every night around this time in his life, this time in Tucson he was currently telling me about, he said they'd start speaking to one another in very civil tones but then it was like some cloud would pass over either him or her and one of them would say something cruel and unforgivable, and then the other person would say something cruel and unforgivable just to keep things balanced, and an argument would ensue, lots of insults and yelling, very personal and private insults and plenty of ugly hoarse yelling, but then right before hanging up they would apologize or at least smooth things over enough so that it'd be clear they would talk again the next night, him under the desert sky, and her under whatever the sky looked like in Baltimore, where she had moved in with her aunt and was working on a novel, a story that would tell us about the childhood of Norman Bates, a story from the mother's point of view.

The bright window of that café. The crimson sofa in that café. And the other crimson sofa.

Franz told me that afternoon at the café that the movie he worked on was a remake of a Fassbinder film, he couldn't remember which one, except it wasn't quite a remake, it simply had some basic ideas from Fassbinder it was playing with, like this woman who sells porn from a wicker basket, that was one, and they did real porn shots which he had never done before, which felt strange filming, this guy and girl in their early twenties, they didn't fuck but he used a large plastic dick on her then she turned it around and put it up his ass, he never knew if they were a couple in real life or just a couple for the film, then at the party after filming they tried to give him the dick and he said no that was all right but they insisted so he stuck it in his bag and flew off to Los Angeles the next day.

Secrets of the Hollywood Hills #3

That afternoon in the café Franz told me money, money, money, that's all he can think about these days. He on the crimson sofa. Myself in the white chair.

He told me money was like trying to catch a butterfly with your bare hands. Or worse. With your mouth while your hands were tied behind your back.

He told me if he had enough money he could make movies that would make Arthur Penn look like shit and Hitchcock look like an idiot, not that he didn't love Penn and Hitchcock.

The blue walls in the café appeared particularly vivid because of the bright windows.

Franz told me that afternoon in the café that one night in Tucson there was this party, him and a bunch of other people on the roof of a house drinking, the stars as big as the ones in that Van Gogh painting, starry starry night or whatever it's called, big fucking stars, stars you'd expect to see at the end of the world, and this one guy, one of the script writers, he was really into Nietzsche and had this elaborate knife collection, Japanese knives with chiseled handles, German knives with ornate and curving blades, and this guy he came up to Franz during this rooftop party and started to say how he could throw Franz off the roof just like that, and he snapped his fingers, and then he said how there was nothing Franz could do about it, but it was his choice the guy said, his choice not to throw Franz off the roof, and he had chosen not to, so Franz didn't have to worry he said, at least not tonight, at least not right now.

Secrets of the Hollywood Hills
#4

Franz said that afternoon at the café that after being robbed last year he never carried money on him, he only used his credit card, but because he was always moving around it was hard to keep up with the statements, it was always a race between one address and the next.

He said Freud thought money was shit: and Marx did too but in a different way.

He said shit was a thing, and he didn't think of money as a thing.

He said money was this ghost, this phantom, who chased him from one place to the next.

Secrets of the Hollywood Hills #5

I ran into Mieze a few months later, she and Franz had finally broken up, I ran into her outside a theater in Chicago, it was cold out, the snow and the night sky made the street look like it was in a black-and-white film, and when I brought up Franz she simply said that jerk, I don't miss him one bit, and she lit up another cigarette.

She said he was helpless, she said he was a forty-three year old who didn't even have an apartment or house of his own, she said he was taking all these pills his quack Los Angles shrink had prescribed for him, they made his eyes have this empty look like the eyes of Norman Bates in the last scene of *Psycho*, the one with the fly on his hand.

She said she had been in Baltimore when he'd been in Tucson and she'd been in Memphis during quite a bit of the time he'd been in Miami.

She said her novel was almost finished but she hadn't come up with just the right ending and she was watching a lot of Fassbinder films, that's all

she seemed to do these days, work at her crappy
job and watch Fassbinder films, because he was
great with endings, like the one where the house
explodes killing off the two main characters or the
one where Petra von Kant's slave calmly leaves Pe-
tra von Kant after a moment of kindness. She said
who understood the tyranny of kindness better
than Fassbinder.

Secrets of the Hollywood Hills #6

Mieze told me that night outside the Chicago theater that she at least had an apartment of her own, she had at least gotten that far in her life if nothing else, at her sister's place it'd always be so awkward every time she brought a guy over, some of them being pretty sleazy, some of them looking like they'd staggered out from a car wreck, their faces full of blankness and bewilderment and meanness.

She said she liked Baltimore better than Tucson though she liked the weather better in Tucson and in fact maybe the best city of all, for her at least, would be a Baltimore that was located in the desert, a Baltimore that stood under a desert night sky.

Secrets of the Hollywood Hills
#7

Mieze told me that night outside the Chicago theater that she never slept with Franz in Tucson because they'd never been in that city at the same time but she had slept with him in Baltimore, three maybe four times, and they'd fucked countless times in Miami which was weird since neither one of them ever lived there.

She said when she finished the first chapter of the novel she walked around Baltimore all night listening to really hard fast jazz, what she liked to call Frenzy Screech Magic Music, music that sounded like it would have been written for the funeral of Antonin Artaud or Charles Baudelaire had this type of jazz existed in their day, but it hadn't of course which somehow in her mind made the music only better, as if she could hear this music that even an Artaud and Baudelaire would not have been able to imagine, not even in the delirium of their death-beds, that's always part of the arrogance of being born later she said, the arrogance and the stupidity, and she walked and walked through the chilly dark night past drug deals and lone guys that whistled at her, she was afraid, really afraid at different points, but she kept on, she kept thinking how if she did live through this night she would remember it very clearly afterwards, it would be like a scene in a film that replays over and over in our dreams.

Secrets of the Hollywood Hills #9

She said her next novel would be about Freud from a pervert's point of view.

She said she would write it on postcards in different parts of the country and then mail those postcards to her mother's address in Memphis and the order of the novel would be based on the order in which she found the postcards in the bowl where her mother kept the mail.

Pastoral Footnotes #1

The hairy shadow vibrated in the embrace of the sticky shadow.

The pink pebbles could well have been the upper half of the face.

The weather, they said, was shit.

The scene, they insisted, was shit.

The budget, they speculated, was fucked.

The script, they realized, was bankrupt.

The characters, they commented, were hazy.

Their bodies, they saw, were oily and skeletal.

Their eyes, they suspected, never closed.

The teeth encircled by billowing purple air.

Pastoral Footnotes #2

We came upon the face later.
It was a spring morning, the grass glittering with dew.
It was a face we loved and thoroughly demolished.
We extracted the bottle from the middle of its head.
The missing part of the face consisted of pink stones.
The mouth chewed its tongue in one film after another.

The weather turned white.
Then the weather turned into salt.
Then the eye turned white.
Then the eye turned into salt.
Then the missing part rested in the salt of the white light.
And turned in the white light of the salt.

The remaining puddle stared at the sky.
The weeds around the puddle glittered.
The bruised neck appeared on screen to thunderous ap-
plause.
The shadow meat flexed its fourth quietest muscle.

The film critic jogged through the park with her dog as the sun lowered behind the trees. The film critic walked through an airport, outside of which was a dark blue sky. The film critic walked through another airport, outside of which was another dark blue sky. The film critic watched a film where children played under a dark blue sky as airplanes occasionally flew overhead. The film critic wondered what Julius Caesar might have looked like in a film, with his hair combed back and a light coating of makeup applied to his face. The film critic told the other film critic that some days she felt exhausted, some days all she wanted to do was stare at one of the movie posters hanging in her apartment for such a long time that all the meaning went away. The film critic ordered an espresso in a café with white chairs and white tables. He scribbled some lines on the back of a postcard, an idea for a film, then he addressed it to his house, and mailed it later that afternoon. The film critic in the last scene of the movie drinks a beer on a plane, outside of which is a dark blue sky.

The Fassbinder Diaries: Day 506

The film critic carries the postcard with a picture of the skeleton from *Psycho* on the front and her theory about the skeleton on the back, written in tiny script. If the skeleton could scream in surprise upon being turned around by the sister of Janet Leigh, what would the scream sound like? The film critic sits in the bath while listening to the couple in the apartment next door make very loud love, though he can't tell if it is actually the couple or a porn film turned up high. The film critic rips up the postcard then scatters the pieces on the café table then stares at them then takes an envelope from her purse and puts them inside and writes her address on the envelope and mails it later that morning.

The Fassbinder Diaries: Day 768

The film critic took a shower and shaved and pulled down the window shades and sat on the bed and thought of pulling down his pajama bottoms and masturbating but decided to try to fall asleep instead. The radio played for an hour but then the electricity went out. Birds were known to kill in certain films and during certain historical eras. The film critic remembered her father as a man walking around the backyard, flashlight in his hand. She thought of her mother as the smell of suntan lotion rising from a damp box in the garage. The film critic watches the scene from *Café Flesh* where the woman being fucked from behind on the luridly lit stage turns her foggy expression toward us. The film critic watches the scene from *Café Flesh* where the man fucking the woman from behind has a jaw like an iron lung. In the shadows past the abandoned drive-in theater stood clumps of bulbous cacti, and in the sunlight behind the parking lot two dogs fought in a haze of pink dust. The film critic watched the lightning strike outside the screen door. She watched the rain and eventually walked out into it. In the movie the branches thrashed around. A shawl had been tied carefully around the trunk, remaining there past the closing credits. The film critic shaved her legs in the bathtub while listening to the radio. The seventh day of April, 1998. The redbud tree in bloom. The film critic sat by his girlfriend in the tub and shaved her legs while they listened to the radio.

Q #1:

Where was Querelle born?

Q #2:

What was his first homosexual encounter?

Q #3:

What was his first heterosexual encounter?

Q #4:

What was his favorite Jean Genet novel?

Q #5:

What was his favorite line from a Douglas Sirk Film?

Q #6:

How did he die?

Q #7:

What was found on his body at the time of death?

Q #8:

What was found in his body at the time of death?

I would like to thank Johannes Goransson and Daniel Bor-
zutzky for helping with their laser-like critical eye. Also, this
book is inspired in part by Michael Gorham's tales of Los An-
geles at its subterranean best.

Made in the USA
Middletown, DE
20 September 2015